Black V

by
Justine Jupe

CHARACTERS
Boy
Jade
Johnnie Johnson
Audrey Nelson
Bonnie Slater
Tanya Matthews

Set: Stage Left: Police Room
Stage Right: Hideout

Action: Summer in a seaside town.

Scene 1

Hideout. JADE enters R followed by BOY.

JADE: *(Looking around)* Is this it? *(BOY just looks at her)* It's different. *(Pause)* Where's the money then?

BOY: Stand still. I want to look at you. Jade isn't it?

JADE: How d'you know. You're an odd one. *(He stares)* Look, I ain't sticking around here. If you ain't got the money, I'm going.

BOY: I haven't started yet.

JADE: *(Glances at him)* You keep a secret?

BOY: What?

JADE: A secret.

BOY: What for? *(Seeing her looking anxious)* Yeah, if you want.

JADE: I get scared.

BOY: Scared? *(Notices her expression)* Sure. So do I sometimes.

JADE: It takes courage, y'know. *(Pause)* It's easy for you.

BOY: You reckon.

JADE: Being a guy an' that. *(Pause as she looks distant; then quickly)* You gonna hand me the money then or not?

BOY: Money? Why should I?

JADE: *(Losing patience)* Sorry, but I ain't hanging around 'ere, it's creepy. Don't know what your problem is...

He grabs her.

BOY: *(Aggressively)* Problem? Like what, eh? Who are you to say? You're the one with the problem, d'you hear.

JADE: Alright, alright, didn't mean nothin' by it. Let go will yer.

BOY: You think I'm odd - don't you?

JADE: Owhh! No.

BOY: That's what you said.

JADE: What?

BOY: Just now. You called me an odd one.

JADE: *(Struggling)* You're hurting. Keep your money, alright. I'll just go.

BOY: What did you mean by odd?

JADE: Nothin'. OK?

BOY: So why say it?

JADE: I dunno. Let go, eh?

BOY: Go? What makes you think I'm going to let you go?

She kicks him. He cries out, letting go. Catching her, he pushes her down. She screams.

BLACKOUT

Scene 2

Police room. TANYA enters followed by JOHNNIE JOHNSON. She walks around nervously.

TANYA: This it, in here? Different from the normal place.

JOHNNIE: This is where Johnnie Johnson usually gets a result. Take a seat.

TANYA: *(Nastily)* No thanks.

JOHNNIE: So what is it that's so important?

TANYA: Depends.

JOHNNIE: Don't mess me about Tanya, I haven't got the time.

TANYA: You got the money?

JOHNNIE: *(Commandingly)* Stand still will you.

TANYA: *(Looking uncomfortable)* You're edgy. *(Pause)* I don't like police stations. If there's no money in it, I'm going.

JOHNNIE: Listen, if you've got information, let's have it.

TANYA: You keep a secret?

JOHNNIE: What?

TANYA: A secret?

JOHNNIE: Stop messing about. *(Sees her looking troubled)* Alright, Tanya, what is it?

TANYA: I don't want anyone to know it was me who told you. I get scared.

JOHNNIE: Scared. What of? *(Pause)* Yeah, right, we all do at sometime.

TANYA: It takes courage, coming here. It's alright for you.

JOHNNIE: You reckon, do you?

TANYA: Being an arrogant copper an' that. *(Pause)* You going to pay me some money then?

JOHNNIE: Money. Why should I? You haven't told me yet.

TANYA: Sorry, but I'm not staying here, it gives me the creeps. If you've got a problem finding out...

She goes to exit but he grabs her.

JOHNNIE: *(Aggressively)* Oh yeah, problem, like what Tanya? Remember, you're the one with the problem, right.

TANYA: *(Softly)* Right. Let go will you.

JOHNNIE: What makes you think I'm edgy, eh?

TANYA: Owhh! That hurts.

JOHNNIE: That's what you said, wasn't it?

TANYA: *(Frightened)* So? Look, keep the money, I just want to get out of here.

JOHNNIE: Not before you tell me what you meant by it.

TANYA: Nothing. Honest.

JOHNNIE: So why say it, eh?

TANYA: I don't know. *(Pause)* Please, let me go.

JOHNNIE: What makes you think I'm going to let you go.

She kicks him.

Right you. *(He pushes her down into a chair)*

She screams.

BLACKOUT

Scene 3

Hideout. BOY arises from bales.

BOY: I don't believe it. I don't know what's the matter with me.

He paces around. JADE half sits, watching him. He finds a packet.

Wanna fag?

JADE: I don't think so.

BOY: Drink?

JADE: In this dump. Where?

BOY: There's a bottle over there... somewhere.

Pause

How old are you?

JADE: Does it matter?

Pause

I said I'd come with yer.

BOY: You what?

JADE: You didn't have to throw me into that filthy truck of yours. And as for those flashing yellow lights... huh, still, was a pick-up truck I suppose. You'll have me mates wondering.

BOY: They'll have seen worse. You always hang around that area?

JADE: What's it to you? *(Pause)* I was waiting for me friend.

BOY: She on the game?

JADE: We were calling on a mate.

BOY: Who's that then?

JADE: That's my business.

Pause

BOY: So why d'you come with me - you didn't fight it.

JADE: 'Cause I like ugly guys, alright!

BOY: *(Going to her)* You watch your mouth!

JADE: Get lost, will yer.

BOY: *(Picking up a bar)* You'd better be careful. I'm not having no 'girl' talk to me like that. I can do you anytime. So just watch it, right! *(He throws the bar down)*

JADE: *(Taken aback)* I told you, I'll be expected back. Me mate saw me getting in your truck.

BOY: Did she see me?

JADE: How do I know.

BOY: Who is she?

JADE: Wouldn't you like to know her number.

BOY is about to threaten her again, but stops.

BOY: What's her name then?

JADE: It'll cost you.

Pause as he thinks about it.

BOY: *(Pulls some money out)* Write it down then.

JADE: Then I want to get out of this smelly hole.

She writes it out and grabs the money.

BOY: I bet you do.

JADE: Don't know why you guys bother if you can't hack it! You weren't half funny. *(She laughs to herself)*

BOY: Shut up will you.

She sees him and can't help laugh some more.

You'd better take that back!

JADE: It was the truth, wasn't it. Anyhow, I'm going.

BOY: Stay there. D'you hear?

JADE: What for? You said I could go.

BOY: I'm keeping you here! *(Picking up bar)* You're staying - get the idea!

He pushes her back down.

BLACKOUT

Scene 4

Station Room. TANYA is sitting in chair, JOHNNIE walks away from her as lights up.

JOHNNIE: I don't believe it. *(Pause)* I don't know what came over me.

He paces around. TANYA follows him with her eyes.

Want a cigarette or something?

TANYA: No.

JOHNNIE: Drink?

TANYA: In this place.

Pause

JOHNNIE: How old are you?

TANYA: Old enough. *(Pause)* I said I'd come in.

JOHNNIE: What?

TANYA: Why send a motor?

JOHNNIE: I like to make sure.

TANYA: *(Sarcastically)* It was a bit embarrassing being bundled into a police car with the siren going and whizzed off in front of my friends.

JOHNNIE: They'll survive. What were you doing hanging around the red light district?

TANYA: Does it matter. *(Pause)* I went to see Jade. She is like a sister y'know.

JOHNNIE: Oh yeah. She working the streets again, I thought she'd given that up.

TANYA: We were visiting a friend, if you know what they are.

JOHNNIE: Anyone we know?

TANYA: That's my business.

Pause

JOHNNIE: So then what happened?

TANYA: Oh, I've forgotten. How sad.

JOHNNIE: *(Going to her)* Don't get cute.

TANYA: Get stuffed!

JOHNNIE: *(He thumps the table so hard she jumps)* Now listen you! It's an offence to withhold evidence. So stop messing about and wasting my time!

TANYA: *(Taken aback)* I told you on the phone. It was a pick-up truck, with black and yellow stripes down the side.

JOHNNIE: And! Then what?

TANYA: I shouted out... I think she saw me... *(Pause)* then I saw this guy push her in, hard.

JOHNNIE: D'you see him?

TANYA: *(Quietly)* I know him.

Silence

JOHNNIE: Well! Who was it?

TANYA gets up and faces him

TANYA: Wouldn't you like to know.

JOHNNIE is about to grab her but thinks better of it.

It'll cost you.

Pause

JOHNNIE: *(Forced calm as he gets some money out)* Alright Tanya.

TANYA: Then I want to get out of this dump.

JOHNNIE: Sure. *(He puts the money down on the desk. She grabs it)*

TANYA: *(Nastily)* It was your own lad, copper. *(She quotes)* "Billy's Breakdown Service" Some service. What a joke! *(She laughs)* Get hooked on that. Bet he 'toed' it fast.

JOHNNIE is stunned. She laughs some more.

JOHNNIE: Shut up will you!

She stops laughing, looking at him nervously.

You'd better not be setting me up.

TANYA: It's the truth! *(Pause)* So, can I go now?

JOHNNIE: Right, come on then.

TANYA: At last!

JOHNNIE: *(Taking her arm)* Let's go see the Custody Sergeant.

TANYA: What for? You said I could go.

JOHNNIE: I'm charging you with soliciting. *(Firmly)* You're staying right here.

TANYA: You gotta be joking.

JOHNNIE: Try me. *(He pushes her out)*

BLACKOUT

Scene 5

Station room: JOHNNIE JOHNSON is sitting on edge of desk. He completes a phone call as AUDREY NELSON enters. He immediately stands up.

AUDREY: *(Walking to desk chair)* Don't get up. Heard you were still here. How many years is it now?

JOHNNIE: Too many. Still, nice to have you back, eh Audrey. The lads said you'd be looking in. You've done well, so they say. *(He takes out a cigarette)*

AUDREY: Not in my presence, remember.

JOHNNIE: *(Sighs)* Yes, I remember. You were just a DS then.

AUDREY: That's right. Same as you Sergeant. Some of us made the career effort despite the male bastions.

JOHNNIE: Feeling antagonized are we?

AUDREY: No Sergeant. Just realistic. You have to be positive and practical to overcome such male orientated obstructions. I do know, believe me. *(Pause)*

JOHNNIE: DI Nelson. Who would have thought.

AUDREY: Not you. That's always been your trouble, though.

JOHNNIE: Pardon Gov.

AUDREY: You call me Ma'am, not Gov. I'm not one of the boys John. Let's have some respect, eh.

JOHNNIE: Respect has to be earned - Ma'am.

AUDREY: Do women disappoint you, Sergeant?

JOHNNIE: They let themselves down.

AUDREY: Women are seldom what men expect them to be.

JOHNNIE: *(Looking her over)* It's not their bodies that are the problem, it's their minds. That's why they'll never break into the male preserve of Chief Constables.

AUDREY: We'll see. But I think you'll find, John, that women are unable to conform to the masculine fantasies of what they should be - thank goodness.

JOHNNIE: Oh yeah, what's that then? Is that why you never had a family?

AUDREY: *(She looks at him for a moment)* Your trouble, Sergeant, is that you like women, but you've got no respect for them, especially if they're in uniform.

JOHNNIE: Put it down to experience - Ma'am.

AUDREY: You might call it experience, others would cry ignorance.

JOHNNIE: Huh, you're the boss.

AUDREY: Exactly, so now I'm here you'll do things my way.

JOHNNIE: Whatever you say.

AUDREY: Let's get one thing straight from the start, shall we, as we'll be working together. I didn't choose to work with you any more than you'd choose to have a female DI. But I shall not tolerate any of your prejudices, Sergeant, despite your 'experience' of women. *(Pause)* Understand?

JOHNNIE: I think I've got the general idea.

AUDREY: Good. *(Looks at him)* So, how's the family?

JOHNNIE: If you mean has anything changed, no. Billy lives with me, and Andrew is still with his mum.

AUDREY: I gather you don't see her anymore.

JOHNNIE: That's about the size of it. Nothing in common. Never did have.

AUDREY: Except for two sons, eh. How is Billy?

JOHNNIE: Runs his own business. Auto - breakdown. At least he's not in this game.

AUDREY: But you are, when we can find you. *(He nods enquiringly)* Down at the desk there's a woman been waiting to see you for over half an hour, but no-one knew where you were. What's going on?

JOHNNIE: Bit of 'private' police business... Ma'am.

AUDREY: Oh?

JOHNNIE: Who is it?

AUDREY: Says she knows you. Refuses to see anyone else.

JOHNNIE: Name?

AUDREY: Bonnie Slater. Mean anything?

JOHNNIE: Our Bonnie. Pain and strife, what's she been up to?

AUDREY: Well let's find out shall we? We'll do this one together, Sergeant.

JOHNNIE: No need for you to bother, Ma'am.

AUDREY: On the contrary, I remember how you used to operate. Go and bring her up. I'll make sure you do it by the book. *(He pulls a face and exits)*

BLACKOUT

Scene 6

AUDREY is seated at the desk as JOHNNIE shows in BONNIE who is very fraught.

JOHNNIE: Over there, Bonnie.

BONNIE: *(Seeing Audrey)* Oh.

AUDREY: Hello Mrs Slater, I'm DI Nelson. Take a seat.

BONNIE: *(To Johnnie)* I wanted to talk to you, luv.

JOHNNIE: It's alright, Bonnie, she's my boss. How times change. Isn't that right... Ma'am.

AUDREY: *(Giving Johnnie a look)* Please relax Mrs Slater. DS Johnson and I have worked together before.

BONNIE: That's as maybe, but... *(She looks at Johnnie who gives her a reassuring nod)*

AUDREY: May I call you Bonnie?

BONNIE: Everyone else round 'ere does.

AUDREY: Right, Bonnie. What is it you wanted to tell us?

BONNIE looks at Johnnie again.

JOHNNIE: Go on sweetheart, it'll be unofficial, OK?

BONNIE: *(Hesitating)* It's my daughter...

AUDREY: What about her?

BONNIE: *(Looks at Johnnie again)* She's gone missing.

JOHNNIE: Your Jade, missing! Huh, so what's new, she's always disappearing.

AUDREY: Sergeant! Bonnie, what makes you think she's 'missing'?

BONNIE: 'Cause I haven't seen her for two days, dear.

JOHNNIE: With all due respect, it'd be more of a surprise to find her at home.

BONNIE: Not this time, chuck.

AUDREY: *(To Johnnie)* You know this girl, do you?

JOHNNIE: A lot of people 'know her', Ma'am.

AUDREY: If what the Sergeant says is correct, what makes you think...

BONNIE: *(Tearfully)* 'Cause today's my birthday, she'd never miss that. Never has, bless her. She said she'd see me this morning, before I opened up, but, but... I mean, I waited as long as I could, but she didn't come, she didn't, so I know something's happened, I know it has, I know it.... *(she breaks down sobbing)*

AUDREY: Alright, Bonnie, take it easy. Let's go over it step by step. *(She indicates to Johnnie to give her a handkerchief for her sniffing)*

JOHNNIE: Here you are love, use this.

BONNIE: Ta. *(Pause)* It's just that she promised you see, promised to be there.

AUDREY: Where was that, Bonnie?

BONNIE: The shop.

AUDREY looks at Johnnie for an explanation.

JOHNNIE: Bonnie does the afternoon shift at Turners. *(Pause)* The newsagents, Ma'am, west end of the promenade.

AUDREY: *(To Bonnie)* Where did you last actually see her?

BONNIE: At the shop, Tuesday evening.

AUDREY: So it wasn't unusual you didn't see her yesterday.

BONNIE: She works at the kennels, at Broad Lane, on a Wednesday.

AUDREY: All day?

BONNIE: Yes, luv.

AUDREY: And in the evening?

BONNIE: Pier Tavern.

JOHNNIE: *(To Audrey)* It's a pub.

AUDREY: *(To Johnnie)* I do remember most things, thank you. *(To Bonnie)* And after the pub shut, were you expecting her home?

JOHNNIE: She doesn't always go home, Ma'am.

AUDREY: Oh, and why is that?

JOHNNIE: Our Bonnie here is her foster mum, aren't you, love? But Jade often stays with friends, so to speak. *(Pause)*

AUDREY: Bonnie?

BONNIE: *(Quietly)* Yes. *(With a pleading look)* Please find her for me. She wouldn't have missed my birthday, not if she was alright.

AUDREY: We will, Bonnie, we will.

BONNIE: She's not a bad kid, not inside. *(Pause)* We've had enough up 'n downs, we have. We had some hard times, enough to make any kid feel they'd lost out. *(Pause)* Before I took her in she must have had a dozen homes, poor mite. Didn't know if she was coming or going. *(Pause)* No roots, see. *(Pause)* I did me best to show her kindness, but maybe I got her too late. You see, Miss, if you've not been used to love, it's hard to show it in return.

JOHNNIE: *(Indicating outside)* Can I have a word, Gov?

AUDREY: *(To Bonnie)* Would you like a cup of tea? *(Bonnie nods)* Right. We won't be a moment. OK? *(Bonnie nods again)*

AUDREY and JOHNNIE exit L and re-enter from wings to downstage spotlight. Semi-fade on Bonnie in room.

AUDREY: I told you not to call me Gov.

JOHNNIE: Oh, yeah, habit I guess.

AUDREY: Well, what is it?

JOHNNIE: We're wasting our time on this one.

AUDREY: I'll decide that, Sergeant.

JOHNNIE: I know most of what goes on around this neighbourhood. Sad though it is, this one has to be a joke. Our Bonnie went through a bad patch after her old man left her and shot back up North. She used to hit the bottle a bit. I think the kid looked after her more than the other way round. Social Services got a file this thick. They're not exactly your reliable family.

AUDREY: Is there such a thing?

JOHNNIE: With respect, Ma'am, do you know what we're looking at here? The 'missing' girl has got a history as a child prostitute. *(A look from Audrey)* Check with the Collator's Office. It's hardly unusual for her sort to disappear, especially in mid-summer in a tourist resort.

AUDREY: 'Her sort', Sergeant. What 'sort' is that?

JOHNNIE: She's a no-hoper, a lost cause. The last thing she needs is us lot turning up, wherever she's hanging out.

AUDREY: Even so, everyone's entitled to be treated seriously. Go back and see her and get an official statement. *(Despairing sigh from JOHNNIE)* Last seen, who with, who her friends are, what sort of places she frequents, what she was wearing, hobbies, the usual. Get Uniform to organise a door to door in the area. Oh, and check the hospitals.

JOHNNIE: What a waste of time and money.

AUDREY: I'll pretend I didn't hear that. *(He looks at her)* I'll leave you to get on with it then. *(She starts to exit L)* And Sergeant, make sure you do it properly. I don't want any corners cut, whatever the history. Just try and think how you would feel if it was your daughter out there. *(She exits)*

JOHNNIE: I'm in more danger than she is.

BLACKOUT

Scene 7

Hideout. JADE is sitting on bales. BOY is drinking from a can.

BOY: Quit staring.

JADE: I'm bored.

BOY: And I'm thinking.

JADE: I need a toilet.

BOY: Tough.

JADE: What you playing at?

BOY: Leave me alone.

JADE: Let me out and I will. *(He doesn't reply)* How come you knew my name? I ain't seen you before.

SILENCE

We ain't hanging around here until you can manage it, are we?

BOY: *(Turning on her)* If you don't keep your mouth shut, I'll shut it for you! *(She recoils)* Bloody questions all the time, why this, why that. Who do you think you are, anyhow? *(Pause)* Look at you. You figure you're so clever, don't you? Getting tarted up in stupid clothes, fancy hair-do and all that make-up - think you get the guys going, poor brainless sods - well not this one. I don't fall for all that hype. You thought I picked you up 'cause I fancied you, right? Ha! What conceit. Take 'em for a ride, do the bit and thanks for the money, sucker. Easy! Well not this one you don't, got it!

JADE: *(Scared)* What you want with me?

BOY: Think I'd bother with a mess like you?

JADE: *(Warily)* What you up to then?

BOY: So smart, eh? Thought you'd got another one. But I got you, see.

JADE: I wasn't trying to...

BOY: You think you're worth paying for? Well, you'll find out how much you're worth. Let's see how long it takes before anyone misses you. Huh, they won't even bother. *(Pause)* That's how much you're worth!

JADE: Can I have a drink? Please.

BOY: I despise your sort. *(Pause)* You encourage people to treat you like dirt. No wonder my dad gets away with it.

He bends down to pick up a canned drink. She dashes out.

Hey!! *(He runs after her)*

BLACKOUT

Scene 8

Downstage spotlight L. JOHNNIE is stood thinking. AUDREY comes in L front wings.

AUDREY: Oh there you are. The missing girl, what's happening?

JOHNNIE: Taken a statement, Gov - sorry, Ma'am. House to house is in progress. No sightings, or at least nobody is owning up to seeing her since yesterday.

AUDREY: Proves my point, Sergeant.

JOHNNIE: What? Oh, maybe. She could be anywhere.

AUDREY: Exactly. Do it my way and we'll find her.

JOHNNIE: Nothings turned up, though.

AUDREY: That's where you're wrong. It has actually, in there.

JOHNNIE: *(Anxiously)* You what?

AUDREY: In the interview room, Sergeant. We've got a witness. Looks like we've got an abduction on our hands. Come on.

FADE SPOTLIGHT DOWNSTAGE. LIGHTS UP ON POLICE ROOM

BONNIE is sitting in chair. TANYA is pacing up and down behind her. AUDREY and JOHNNIE enter.

JOHNNIE: *(To Tanya)* What are you doing here?

AUDREY: *(Sitting down at desk)* You arrested her. She's a friend of Jade Slater, didn't you realise? She informed the Custody Sergeant she was a witness to this. *(JOHNNIE looks worried)* Turn the tape on. *(He switches recorder on)*

Wednesday, June 29th. 2.32pm. Interview between Mrs Bonnie Slater, Tanya Matthews, Detective Sergeant Johnson and Detective Inspector Nelson. *(She clears her throat)* Mrs Slater has declined a solicitor, and is acting as guardian for Tanya Matthews, both of whom are here voluntarily.

JOHNNIE: *(To TANYA)* Is this connected with this morning? *(TANYA ignores him)*

AUDREY: A statement has already been obtained from Mrs Slater, who today reported that the girl she fostered, Jade Slater, was missing. Tanya Matthews witnessed an incident involving a girl she recognised as Jade Slater, who was seen being bundled into a yellow and black truck, which was then driven off at speed heading west towards Bluestone sands at Barley. Tanya, is that correct?

TANYA: Yes.

AUDREY: Did you see the driver? Could you describe him?

TANYA: Yes, miss. *(Looks at JOHNNIE)* Reminded me of someone.

JOHNNIE: What time was this?

TANYA: About 11 o'clock.

JOHNNIE: You never told me.

TANYA: *(She looks at him - hesitates)* No.

AUDREY: You saw Sergeant Johnson about this incident?

TANYA: Yeah. So what?

AUDREY: And you never mentioned it?

TANYA: No.

AUDREY: Even though Jade is like a sister to you?

TANYA: What she gets up to is her business.

AUDREY: Really. *(Pause)* Sergeant?

JOHNNIE: Tanya Matthews refused to talk, Ma'am.

TANYA: Bleeding right, I did.

AUDREY: And why would that be?

JOHNNIE: *(Together)* She wanted money, too much...
TANYA: ⎱   He threatened me. He said that....

AUDREY: Hold it!! *(Pause)* Sergeant, is this true? This girl came to see you this morning, and you....

JOHNNIE: Not specifically about this, Ma'am.

AUDREY: Oh?

JOHNNIE: I didn't know about this then. Not for certain.

AUDREY: So what exactly was it about, Tanya?

JOHNNIE: She had other information.

AUDREY: I'm asking Tanya. Well?

TANYA: *(Quietly)* He's lying.

JOHNNIE: I'm lying? Hah, come on, Ma'am, she's a Matthews. That lot lie through their teeth.

BONNIE: Why don't you hear her out, Chuck, you might learn summin'.

JOHNNIE: When I need your advice, Bonnie, I'll bring a bottle.

TANYA: *(Upset)* He did know about it, 'cause I phoned him. I told him what I'd seen, Jade being forced into this breakdown truck, and that I recognised the driver. He said to come and see him, he'd make it worth my while. I need the money, see. When I wouldn't tell him, he threatened me, right here in this room.

AUDREY: Threatened you? With what?

TANYA: *(Crying)* He was going to charge me with soliciting. To buy himself time and keep me quiet. I'd never get money that way, never.

BONNIE: *(Going to comfort her)* Alright luv, take it easy.

JOHNNIE: Here come the tears. It's more predictable than Bank Holiday rain.

BONNIE: You could show some feeling, you... you *pig*!

JOHNNIE: Spare me the pleasantries, please.

AUDREY: *(To Johnnie)* Well?

JOHNNIE: I didn't believe Miss Matthews when she phoned, and I don't now.

But I had reason to believe she might have other information relating to what she claimed she had seen. When she refused this information, it was time to put a bit of pressure on.

AUDREY: This is your normal method, is it, by threats?

JOHNNIE: I find it usually works on the weaker sex... Ma'am.

AUDREY: Go on.

JOHNNIE: She claimed the breakdown vehicle she'd seen belonged to my lad, Billy. *(Pause)*

AUDREY: Well?

JOHNNIE: I checked immediately on his movements. He's clean. He was in Birmingham today. *(With a look at Tanya)* A long way from the beach. The DCI will verify it, Ma'am.

AUDREY: Maybe he will. *(She stops - then to Bonnie and Tanya)* Excuse us, we won't be a moment. Interview suspended. *(She indicates outside to Johnnie)* Tape, Sergeant. *(He switches the tape off and follows her out)*

FADE ON ROOM. LIGHTS UP DOWNSTAGE.

AUDREY: As I was about to say, what worries me, Sergeant, is you suppressing this information whilst you have it checked out, during which time you knew that a young girl could be in danger.

JOHNNIE: She was no more in danger than that one was of telling the truth. How you going to prove that someone with Jade Slater's record didn't go willingly?

AUDREY: I hope you're right. Perhaps with your 'experience' of women, you can tell me why Miss Matthews should make it all up?

JOHNNIE: Girls like her don't need a reason, it's a way of life.

AUDREY: Well let me tell you, Sergeant Johnson, I know when a woman's tears are real.

JOHNNIE: Who's under question here? Bloody women, they know when to....

AUDREY: *(Command)* You'll hear me out! Whatever the truth here, you have been negligent in following down procedure. What is more, you have put your own personal problems before that of a person suspected of having been abducted, and failed to act immediately on a witnesses' report. Worse, you 'interviewed' Miss Matthews without her having a guardian present. In short, Sergeant, you've let everybody down, including yourself.

JOHNNIE gets out a cigarette, but a 'look' from Audrey stops him.

Right. Let's continue, shall we?

They go back into the room. REVERT LIGHTING. JOHNNIE switches the tape back on.

(To Bonnie and Tanya) Interview resumed. I shall order a full investigation into this.

BONNIE: That won't help find my daughter.

AUDREY: Pardon?

BONNIE: Investigating him.

AUDREY: *(To Tanya)* You said you could describe the driver of the truck.

TANYA: *(Thinks for a moment)* About 6 foot, slim, short blond hair. ....type of jacket/jeans/shoes***

JOHNNIE: Well that isn't my Billy.

AUDREY: I don't suppose you noticed the number of the...

TANYA: *(Suddenly)* Tell you what, it was facing that way, and he pushed her in from the pavement, then walked round the front, so it must be a left hand drive.

JOHNNIE: *(Reacting)* You sure?

TANYA: Jade can't handle a set of wheels.

The telephone rings. AUDREY answers it.

AUDREY: Yes. Speaking. Where? Right, thanks. *(She puts the receiver down)* They've got a fix. Samwell's Farm, up near Dissett Bay. Helicopter spotted the truck.

JOHNNIE: Helicopter! - for this job. Where did that come from?

AUDREY: From our budget. I ordered it. I saw the Super. I do the job properly, Sergeant.

JOHNNIE: Women, where would we be without them.

AUDREY: *(To Johnnie)* Get over there and sort it. Oh, keep County informed as it's their area. Better take Mrs Slater with you as well. By the way, you'll need a coat, apparently it's chucking it down.

JOHNNIE: That's all I need. *(Switches tape off)* Summer by the sea! *(To Bonnie, with a sigh)* Let's go find her then.

BONNIE: *(To Audrey)* Thank you. I knew you'd do it. *(To Tanya)* Come on, love.

BONNIE and TANYA exit.

JOHNNIE: *(To Audrey)* What d'you reckon?

AUDREY: I don't like the sound of this one.

JOHNNIE: What are we dealing with?

AUDREY: No details yet. Could be a siege situation. It's unpredictable.

JOHNNIE: Surprise me. *(Pause)* Tactical Firearm Unit?

AUDREY: No. Assess the situation first. No stampede heroics, eh John.

JOHNNIE: *(As he exits)* Yes, Ma'am.

AUDREY: I only hope you're in time - for your sake.

He gives her a 'look'.

BLACKOUT

Scene 9

Hideout - Empty.

BOY: *(Shoving Jade in)* Get back in there.

They're both wet.

JADE: You let go! What's the point? *(She rubs her arms)* I'm soaking.

BOY: You shouldn't have gone out there, should you? *(He picks up his packet of cigarettes. It's empty. He crumples it in disgust)* You try that again and I'll turn you over.

JADE: *(Sarcastically)* You can't keep me here.

BOY: You'll do as I say, got it!

JADE: *(Rubbing her arms)* I'm cold.

BOY: Quit moaning will you.

JADE: Very impressive. So now what, tough guy?

BOY: *(Gruff)* You got any smokes?

JADE: No. Not that sort.

BOY: *(Grabbing her handbag)* Let's have a look.

JADE: Get off!

He snatches it, turns away from her, delves inside the bag to look. She jumps him. They struggle. He pushes her off, looks in the bag, finds nothing. He hurls it down in disgust, kicks out an object. He looks back, then he notices she is groaning.

BOY: *(Goes to her, concerned)* What's up? Jade? What you doing? *(With gasping intakes she tries to get her breath) (Frightened)* What is it?

She passes out.

(Panicky) Jade? Come on. I didn't mean this. Honest. Jade!! *(He gets up - to himself)* You stupid burke, you. *(He suddenly starts tidying up, putting things neatly. He sees her handbag and puts the items back in. He hears her coming round; going to her)* You alright? Jade? *(He helps her)* Come on, sit here. *(He helps her onto a bale)* What happened?

JADE: *(Holding twixt rib and abdomen)* Your elbow or something, right here.

BOY: *(Wrapping his jacket around her shoulders)* Here.

JADE: That bleeding hurt.

BOY: You gonna be OK?

JADE: You got any drink left?

BOY: Sure. *(He gets it - she drinks)*

JADE: That's better.

BOY: What am I doing.

JADE: What?

BOY: I don't know why I'm doing this. *(Looks at her)* You OK?

JADE: I've felt better.

BOY: Here - here's your bag.

JADE: *(Taking it)* I have got some smokes somewhere. *(She looks and finds them)*

BOY: I don't suppose...

JADE: Yeah, why not. *(They both light up)* What's yer name?

BOY: Andy. Look, I'm sorry. I can't believe I've done this.

JADE: So why did yer?

BOY: *(Big sigh)* To... to prove something, I think.

JADE: *(Wryly)* Well, you're certainly not the normal punter.

BOY: It hurtin' still?

JADE: You ain't the person I thought you was. *(Pause)* Look, I ain't into confessionals, but you been here before?

BOY: *(Quietly)* Yes... 'cause it's sort of private, and derelict.

JADE: I can see that!

BOY: *(Serious)* I can be myself here. Well, not like just now; but on my own - no interference. A few fags, cans, bit of music.

JADE: So why drag me along? *(Pause)*

BOY: I come from a broken home.

JADE: Who doesn't?

BOY: My dad took my brother, and mum got me. That's my brother's truck outside.

JADE: So what you doing with it?

BOY: He's in Birmingham. He gave me a job. I help out now and then.

JADE: Like this?

BOY: Sorry. *(Pause)* Our Billy was always my Dad's favourite. Good at sports, works for himself, got a bit of money and that, goes drinking, lots of girlfriends - not like me. I envied him.

JADE: *(With the drink)* Want some?

BOY: Thanks. *(He sips - hands it back)* Not 'cause he was good at things, but because I was with mum. Dad hated me like he hated her. I wanted to be like him too. I told him once, but he laughed.

JADE: What's he do?

BOY: He's a copper.

JADE: What!! You're jokin'.

BOY: No - he's a good one at that. *(Pause)* I just wanted him to accept me, to recognise me, as I am. But I'm not tough enough for him. He sees me as a mummy's boy.

JADE: So?

BOY: So I tried to be like Billy. He was smart with girls, they liked him. He said to me once, it's not what you are, but what they think you are. He could live like that, but not me.

JADE: It takes all sorts, I'll tell yer.

BOY: I was confused. Mum always said treat girls with love and care but dad said girls liked to be treated rough.

JADE: We've all been there. My mates used to say you gotta have sex or the guy won't love yer, so I figured sex meant love - but it don't.

BOY: Girls could tell I was false, acting up tough. So I didn't bother. I couldn't stand getting rejected, it was like my dad all over again. I wanted to be with them, but they didn't like me. I was an outsider.

JADE: Then?

BOY: I suppose I made up my own world, y'know, magazines, pictures, even videos. I used to dress up, you can be what you want then, there's no-one to reject it. Billy used to say get 'em young, they're naive, but I never had the nerve to even ask a schoolgirl out, in case they laughed and thought I was... I dunno, a pervert or something.

JADE: No, they come in suits. And all this?

BOY: Girls doing what you do don't say no.

JADE: And guys don't go to all this trouble either.

BOY: *(Awkwardly)* I only thought... I mean... I wanted to prove to them; prove I could do something they wouldn't have the guts to do... but just now, you lying there and that, it was stupid. I shouldn't have to prove anything to them.

JADE: Your world's more of a mess than mine!

BOY: Tell you what, I shan't forget you.

JADE: I won't have a problem with that. *(Pause - looks around)* So, is there a loo?

BOY: Oh, yeah, forgot. Out round the back there's a shed type thing.

JADE: Don't suppose you've got an umbrella in this 'house' of yours?

He shrugs as she exits. He gets up and calls out.

BOY: I'll give you a lift back though!

He walks around, then sits again, back to door, thinking. JOHNNIE JOHNSON enters.

(Hearing a noise half turns his head) If only I hadn't...

JOHNNIE: Come on lad, you can either come quietly or...

BOY turns round to look.

Oh not you. What the hell are you doing here!? For pity's sake, Andrew, what you playing at messing around with that tramp - don't you know any better, haven't you got any bloody sense.

BOY: She's not a...

JOHNNIE: You got any idea of the trouble we've gone to over this? You crazy or just pure stupid? D'you know what you've done? Your dad's a copper - didn't you even think of that?

BOY: At least she listen's to me! She's done more for me in five minutes than you ever did.

JOHNNIE: Good was it? You poor sod - you're just like your mum.

BOY: When it comes to people's feelings you haven't got a clue - why did I ever want to impress you!

JOHNNIE: I'm your father, aren't I?

BOY: How I wish I had one.

JADE enters.

JADE: *(As a question)* My handbag over there...

JOHNNIE: Who let you back in? Get out of here you stupid cow!

BOY pulls her over towards him.

BOY: Don't you talk to her like that.

JOHNNIE: No good hiding behind skirts all your life.

BOY: I'm not.

JOHNNIE: *(Moving towards them)* Listen, boy, don't be a fool. She's no protection. I'll 'take her out' if I have to. She's not worth a spit.

BOY: What would you know about friendship.

JOHNNIE: Don't be so bloody soft.

BOY: Oh, is this how you prefer it. *(He picks up the bar)*

JOHNNIE: Now come on, sonny, be sensible. I've come in solo, but you're surrounded out there.

BOY: I'll not be taken in by the likes of you.

JOHNNIE: *(To Jade)* Out the way, you.

As he pulls Jade to one side, BOY hits him with the bar. JOHNNIE falls to the ground. BOY raises the bar to strike again.

BOY: To each his own!!

JADE: Don't! *(JADE grabs for the bar)*

BLACKOUT

Scene 10

Station room. Enter BONNIE, JADE, TANYA and AUDREY. They all sit.

AUDREY: I've called you all in here because as you refused to have a solicitor, I need to advise you on your options, Mrs Slater, as you are their legal guardian, and because of the peculiarities of this case.

BONNIE: I don't understand it all.

AUDREY: Well, are you going to prefer charges?

JADE: No!!

BONNIE: *(To Jade)* Look what he put you through. He's an animal.

TANYA: The real leopard is out there.

JADE: He's no animal, just misunderstood - like most of us.

BONNIE: I need to think.

AUDREY: *(Waits for a moment)* In that case I have to tell you that Sergeant Johnson has stated that if you *don't* press charges against Andrew Johnson, the Sergeant intends to charge you.

BONNIE: Who?

AUDREY: All of you, Mrs Slater.

TANYA: Give over, what have we done?

AUDREY: I'm sorry, Bonnie. *(Looks at Jade)* I have no choice. *(Pause)* He wants you to charge his son with 'abduction with intent to incite a minor'.

TANYA: We're more likely to incite him, from what I heard.

BONNIE: I see. He gets to look the honourable bobby insisting his son gets put down, yet all the time he doesn't like him anyway.

AUDREY: As I was saying, it's either that, or charging you.

BONNIE: With what?

SILENCE

AUDREY: Well... both Jade and Tanya here with soliciting, and you with living off immoral earnings.

BONNIE: *(Getting up)* Who does this character think he is? Don't you think my girls have been through enough? What is this anyway, I thought you were in charge. He can't make accusations just like that.

AUDREY: Please sit down.

BONNIE: No, I bloody won't!

AUDREY: Mrs Slater, you must understand that Sergeant Johnson must have evidence of this, otherwise he wouldn't be in a position...

TANYA: *(Interrupting)* To threaten us again.

BONNIE: You can tell that so called 'Sergeant' of yours to leave my girls alone. I've never heard the like.

AUDREY: This is not helping, Mrs Slater.

BONNIE: Well, what you expect, coming out with such tripe. Living off immoral earnings indeed. What's he think we are?

AUDREY: I think you'll find, my dear, that...

BONNIE: Don't you patronise me.

JADE: *(Quietly)* Ma. *(BONNIE looks round to Jade)* Ma - it's true.

TANYA: Speak for yourself 'sister'.

BONNIE: What's true?

JADE: I've been earning Ma... like he says.

BONNIE looks to Audrey, then Jade, then to Tanya.

TANYA: *(Getting up)* Don't look at me, she said it.

JADE: *(To Tanya; gets up)* You ain't so clean, you two faced snout.

TANYA: At least I'm street legal.

JADE: *(Grabs Tanya)* And yer money is as dirty as yer mouth.

TANYA: You should know!

BONNIE: Quiet!! I didn't bring you up to behave like this.

JADE: *(Goes to her)* Sorry. Oh, I'm so sorry.

BONNIE: Leave me alone. Give me a minute.

AUDREY: I apologise Bonnie, that you should have to find out like this.

TANYA: *(To Bonnie)* Please listen to me. We didn't mean to upset you like this, it's just that, well, you've worked hard all your life, and for what? You've given youngsters like us a home, despite your own problems, made us feel secure by showing us that being thoughtful and loving is what matters. We'll always love you, because you taught us how.

BONNIE: That would have been enough.

Pause

TANYA: What we've done we did for the money. You'll always have love, from us, but you've never had much money. What we gave you came from... well, Jade you know about now. And mine came from giving information - to the police. Never again though, not after what that louse has tried to do.

BONNIE: I also tried to tell you that it pays to be honest.

JADE: *(Looks at Tanya)* We have been honest - with ourselves.

SILENCE

BONNIE: You two! I don't know. Chalk and cheese. I feel I ought to... but, *(with a sigh)* I done my bit. It's your life now. You always were full of surprises. *(Pause)* I knew you'd show for my birthday - sometime!

JADE: We'd never miss that, Ma.

BONNIE hugs Jade and Tanya.

AUDREY: Mrs Slater, Bonnie, you'll have to decide. Do you want us to charge Andrew Johnson?

BONNIE looks at the girls, then turns to Audrey.

BONNIE: The law is all black and white, isn't it? Yes or no. One or the other has to be guilty and not guilty. There's never any allowance made for unusual circumstances...

AUDREY: There's a reason for most things.

BONNIE: There doesn't have to be a motive when someone makes a mistake. *(Pause)* As far as we are concerned, Andrew Johnson can go home.

AUDREY: Thank you Bonnie. *(As she exits)* Excuse me.

FADE LIGHTS ON STATION ROOM. LIGHTS UP DOWNSTAGE. Sergeant Johnson is waiting. AUDREY comes to him.

AUDREY: There you are.

JOHNNIE: Well, what's the verdict?

AUDREY: No charges.

JOHNNIE: Told you - they're losers. Right! Got 'em.

AUDREY: Just a moment. You have made sure your evidence will hold up?

JOHNNIE: They'll have a job proving otherwise, won't they?

AUDREY: And your son?

JOHNNIE: Son? I'd given up on him years ago.

AUDREY: That's been the problem.

JOHNNIE: You'd know all about the family, wouldn't you, Ma'am.

AUDREY: What I'm getting at, Sergeant, is that if you charge *them* and not your Andrew, don't you think it will come out that he got off because he's the son of a policeman?

JOHNNIE: Advice from a woman?

AUDREY: It's up to you. After all, vanity is man's Achilles heel.

JOHNNIE: So? Where will that leave me?

AUDREY: Exactly. I should think about it if I was you, eh Sergeant?

THE END

STAGE PLAN

Stage L - **Police Room**   Stage R - **Hideout**

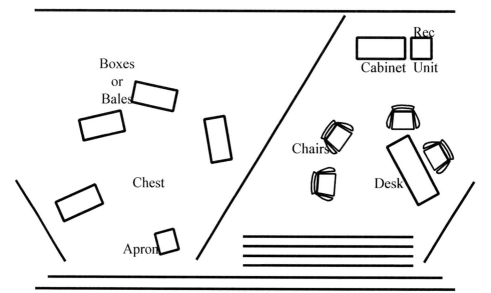

Author's notes

A small, self-operating blue strobe located up stage centre can be very effective with the blackout as the tabs open.

The apron should be utilised for the confrontations between the D.I. and the Sergeant, with the set in blackout.

The junk in the hideout can overflow into the police room, suggesting a link between the two aspects, whilst the lighting can be used to effectively divide the two areas.

This play was first performed at the Woking Drama Festival.

LIGHTING

Cue	Page	Scene	
0	2	Open	Open main tabs to blackout
1	2	1	*Up* LEFT
2	3	2	*Fade* LEFT, *up* RIGHT
3	5	3	*Fade* RIGHT, *up* LEFT
4	7	4	*Fade* LEFT, *up* RIGHT
5	9	5	*Fade* RIGHT, then *up* RIGHT again
6	11	6	*Fade* RIGHT, then *up* RIGHT again
7	14	6	*Fade* RIGHT, *up* APRON *cross spot L to R*
8	15	7	*Fade* APRON, *up* LEFT
9	16	8	*Fade* LEFT, *up* APRON
10	16	8	*Fade* APRON, *up* RIGHT
11	19	8	*Fade* RIGHT, *up* APRON
12	20	8	*Fade* APRON, *up* RIGHT
			Music 9 seconds
13	21	9	*Fade* RIGHT *up* LEFT
14	26	10	*Hold 8 seconds*, then *fade* LEFT, *up* RIGHT
15	29	10	*Fade* RIGHT, *up* APRON
16	29	End	*Fade* APRON to full blackout & curtain

PROPERTIES

Police Room: Desk
Four chairs
Telephone
Waste bin
Tape unit
optional: Filing cabinet
Radiator
Small table

Hideout: Chest
Straw bales or sacking
Wooden boxes
Broken chair
Metal pole
General rubbish, used cans, cigarette packets, bottles, magazines, etc.

Personal

Jade: handbag, cigarettes, matches, pencil & scrap paper

Boy: cigarette packet, money, canned drink, jacket

Johnnie: money, cigarettes, lighter, handkerchief, raincoat, plaster

Bonnie: old shopping bag

Tanya: handbag

Audrey: briefcase & notes